TSFR:

THE TAOIST WAY TO TOTAL SEXUAL FITNESS—FOR MEN

by Bruce M. Wong

Library of Congress Catalog Card Number: 82-99881
ISBN: 0-910295-00-X

PUBLISHED BY:
Golden Dragon Publishers, Inc.
P.O. Box 1529
Princeton, New Jersey 08540

To the ancient Taoist who originally developed TSFR.

CONTENTS

INTRODUCTION

You are about to discover–and learn to use–a technique for total male sexual fitness rarely known in the western world. Developed thousands of years ago by the ancient Chinese followers of Lao-tzu, the founder of Taoism, it is a technique that has been privately passed down from father to son for countless generations. It has never been shared publicly. Even today it is known to only a limited number of Chinese, many of whom treat it as a closely guarded secret.

The technique is called the Taoist Sexual Fitness Regimen, or "TSFR," and as far as can be determined, this is the first published work concerning it. Over the centuries, however, various practitioners of TSFR have committed their special knowledge to paper in the form of handwritten notes and observations. The information in this manual is based upon several sets of these privately held notes, all of which were traced, translated, and verified by the author over a period of several years.

The Taoist Sexual Fitness Regimen has been shown to be an effective technique for overcoming and preventing impotence, increasing staying power, and generally improving a male's overall sexual fitness and enjoyment. It has worked for countless Chinese fortunate enough to have received TSFR instruction. In fact, the author has many years of gratifying personal experience of practicing this Taoist regimen. It will work for you.

To enable us to refine TSFR even further, however, we have initiated a project to collect personal experiences, tips, and advice from TSFR users. The survey at the end of this publication is designed for this purpose, and we hope you will take a moment or two to fill it out and mail it in (anonymously) at an appropriate time. The information you provide can be an invaluable aid to others who are interested in improving their sexual fitness. And it will enable us to provide even more information on TSFR in the future.

The Taoist Sexual Fitness Regimen is too important to be kept a secret any longer. The sexual self-confidence it makes possible, the increased pleasure, and the joy it can bring to both partners in a sexual relationship must be shared. Clearly the time has come for someone well-versed in Taoist sexual techniques to provide the necessary information. If by doing so it is possible to bring more love and happiness to mankind in a very natural and essential way, then this publication will have achieved its goal.

Bruce Wong

Princeton, New Jersey
November, 1981

4

PART I: Sexual Fitness Through TSFR

The "Way" of TSFR

TSFR is a mental and physical exercise program designed to maximize male sexual fitness. Based upon the ancient teachings of Taoism, a widespread Chinese philosophy that emphasizes naturalness, spiritual freedom, and above all the tao (pronounced: "dow," literally: the "way"), TSFR can enable a male to both achieve an erection and maintain it through the sexual stimulation of prolonged intercourse. There is also some evidence to show that TSFR naturally stimulates production of the male hormone (testosterone) which can result in increased sexual drive.

Mastering TSFR does require a certain amount of concentrated effort and practice. However, once you have become proficient, maintaining your sexual fitness at its peak requires only a few minutes of simple exercises each day.

There is nothing "mystical" about TSFR as it is presented here. All non-relevant material has been systematically eliminated. What remains is the essence of TSFR: a set of dynamic, time-proven exercises that–combined with the proper mental approach–can increase and maintain male sexuality. In this sense, the logic behind TSFR is indisputable.

Increasing the strength, endurance, and efficiency of any part of your body requires regular exercise. Indeed, the general rule in overall physical fitness is, "If you don't use it, you lose it." Why shouldn't the same rule apply to the sex-related parts of one's body?

Well, of course, the same rule does apply. The difference is that sex–unlike other forms of physical activity–is still something of a taboo subject, making detailed information on specific exercises concerning it relatively difficult to find. Besides, sex is supposed to be something one knows how to do "naturally," without practice or instruction. But, of course, just because someone "naturally" knows how to throw a baseball doesn't make him a major league pitcher.

TSFR can't promise to instantly catapult you into the "major leagues"–no responsible program can. But it can provide you with the tools you need to overcome impotence, prevent premature ejaculation, and generally improve your sexual performance. The rest is up to you.

Let's look first at the problems of impotence and premature ejaculation. Then we'll see how TSFR in both its original and modified versions acts to effectively overcome them.

The Problem of Impotence

One of the most common and frustrating sexual problems a man can face is impotence–the regular failure to achieve or maintain an erection.[1] It's important to point out that impotence doesn't necessarily involve loss of the sexual desire. On the contrary, it is frustrating and humiliating precisely because one wishes for sex but can not, for one reason or another, succeed.

Impotence can be partial or total. Many men have experienced both forms at one time or another in their adult lives. Loss of sexual potency can and does strike men of all ages. It is far from being a problem limited to older men.[2] Stress,

1. Lawrence E. Lamb, M.D., Editor, "Impotence", The Health Letter, Vol. III No. 12, 1974, Communications Inc., P.O. Box 326, San Antonio, Texas 78292.
2. Ibid.

tension, and many pressures of modern life undoubtedly have an effect on man's sexual life. Excessive use of tobacco, too much alcohol or drugs, worry about one's job, concern about family finances, depression, and fatigue all contribute to the decline of a man's sexual capacity.[3]

There are, of course, other factors, such as a lack of hormones, damage to the nerve reflex mechanism, or poor circulation due to fatty cholesterol deposits in the arteries over the body of the testicles, diabetes, etc. that could be the causes of impotence.[4] Besides these kinds of diseases or injuries, the impotence could also be caused by psychological factors.[5]

The Myth of Male Menopause

The percentage of impotence rises rapidly after the age of 50. This problem is often referred to as middle-aged impotence. Sometimes, it is even mistaken for a male menopause.[6] This is the result of widespread misinformation, a belief that declining male sexual activity and potency is a natural part of aging. Actually, aging has very little to do with genuine impotence. Neither men nor women

---

3. Lamb, op. cit.
4. Ibid.
5. Ibid.
6. John Chesterman & Michael Marten, *Man to Man*, Berkley Publishing Corporation, New York, 1978, p. 235.

lose either sexual function or sexual desires with age. Men with a healthy life style often retain their sexual capacity to 100 years of age or longer.[7] A fit and healthy man should, in theory, be able to have intercourse at any age. The Abkhasian men of the Cacusus of Russia, to cite one example, commonly remain sexually active to 100 years of age.[8] These men stay lean, don't smoke, and remain physically active.

Because of the kind of misconception and misunderstanding mentioned above, many men with impotence problems try to pretend that it is "normal" at their age. When the problem persists the sufferer eventually begins to convince himself that the inability to get an erection–or at best to get only a partial one–is something that he has to accept and live with. As a result, the sufferer's pride is hurt and his self-image and his behavior are affected. He might feel depressed and a sense of hopelessness.

Middle-aged impotence is a relatively common problem that may be caused by too much alcohol or drugs, too much tobacco, anxiety and fatigue, etc. It may arise at the age of 35, 40, 45, etc. It is simply not "menopausal." In short, the idea that any fit and healthy man must put up with reduced

7. Lamb, op. cit.
8. Ibid.

sexual vigor and loss of erectile capacity is simply not true.

The Problem of Premature Ejaculation

Premature ejaculation is defined as ejaculation before the man desires it and before fulfilling the sexual desires of either partner. It is a very common problem experienced by men of all ages. It is not just a problem of young men who have this trouble because of lack of experience. Older men with weak potency also have this trouble. Most men experienced premature ejaculation one time or another in their sex lives.

The problem commonly encountered during intercourse is that he can not keep himself from ejaculating long enough for his partner to achieve orgasm. The frustration and anxiety caused by premature ejaculation are felt by both partners, as it is so vividly demonstrated by one male's comment: "It makes me feel like such a flop when she's begging me to keep it just a little longer and I'm failing her." Indeed, as Dr. S. A. Kaufman has pointed out in a recent book on the subject, the sex problem most women complain about most often is the failure to reach orgasm during intercourse.[9]

9. Sherwin A. Kaufman, M.D., *Sexual Sabotage: How Physical and Emotional Problems Can Undermine Your Sex Life*, MacMillan, Inc., 1981.

And, of course, premature ejaculation on the part of the male is frequently responsible.

Conventional Solution to Both Problems

In the past there was little that could be done to solve these frustrating sexual problems. Many sufferers in desperation were forced to resort to hormone therapy, to taking various kinds of "aphrodisiacs," or to seeking help from a psychoanalyst. Some even use "sexual aids" like the "cock ring" to achieve and maintain an erection.[10]

While hormone therapy may benefit certain people if it is the real cause of the problem, there are possible side effects from this treatment. Besides, the problem is usually not caused by the lack of sufficient amounts of male hormone (testosterone). In fact, taking male hormone can turn off your own natural supply and it can make things worse.

As far as various kinds of commercial aphrodisiacs are concerned, some might be able to give the effect of temporary booster but they could be addictive and there are undesirable side effects associated with using this kind of drug, too. Repeated uses of aphrodisiacs or sex creams could result in a psychological block in the user's mind to

10. Chesterman & Marten, op. cit.

rely on the drugs and to lose natural physical ability. So the condition gets worse rather than better. The effectiveness of a "cock ring," like any sex aid, depends on the user's attitude toward it. Some people find it uncomfortable and irritating, while others are aroused by the constant stimulation of the device.[11] It is obvious that these kinds of treatments are not really effective. Besides, they are unnatural.

For those who do not have impotence problems, there is an equally important question of what can be done to prevent such problems from developing. The general advice one receives about this question is that a man can do a lot to prevent impotence by following the common good health rules and by keeping himself physically fit.

But this kind of general advice won't help people much. What is really needed is specific instruction. Common sense is fine as far as it goes, but it rarely goes far enough.

For both the problems of impotence and premature ejaculation, there is another answer: The Taoist Sexual Fitness Regimen.

11. Chesterman & Marten, op. cit.

What is the Taoist Sexual Fitness Regimen?

As mentioned earlier, TSFR is a special form of exercise. It includes procedures for flexing the penis and strengthening the physical system which controls the tightening of the anus, the genitals, and bladder outlet. These procedures and exercises are complemented by a set of special massages designed to stimulate and tone up certain parts of the body.

Continued practice of both the massages and the exercises can enable a man to reinforce his gonadal region, to naturally stimulate the production of male hormone (testosterone), to increase the "muscle-like" tone of his penis, to gain first-class erection, and to delay and control his ejaculation during intercourse. The developed ability to control ejaculation through TSFR will enable you to prevent premature ejaculation and to help your partner achieve orgasm or even multiple orgasms.

In other words, continued practice of TSFR will enable one to stay sexually fit at all times. Sexual fitness is defined as a person's ability to perform his sexual function at a high level of efficiency. It includes strength, endurance, and general sexual capacity.

Like yoga, the martial arts, and other oriental exercise programs, TSFR is an activity that is both physical and "spiritual"–or "psychological" in more modern terms. It is thus intended to act upon both the body and the mind as an integrated whole. This is important, for it means that TSFR will not only enable you to strengthen your sexual potency but also to gain complete self-confidence in your ability to perform effectively. After all, fear of failure ranks high among the psychological factors responsible for impotence.[12]

TSFR provides anyone currently suffering from impotence or premature ejaculation with what is probably the most effective and natural way to overcome their problems and reinvigorate their sexual power. No drugs, medicine, or conventional medical or psychological treatment is required.

There is only one exception. If a man is not able to obtain an erection (not even a partial erection) at any time at all (not even during sleep, for example) he is impotent because of certain real diseases or physical injuries. In such cases, proper medical diagnosis and treatment are clearly indicated. TSFR alone will not be effective.

TSFR is for Everyone

It should be stressed that the benefits of TSFR are not limited to men suffering from impotence or

---

12. Lamb, op. cit.

premature ejaculation. Following the program is probably the best thing anyone can do to achieve and maintain sexual fitness. The physical system that controls the sexual function grows in strength, endurance, and flexibility with increased exercise as prescribed in TSFR.

Of course, in the broader sense, sexual fitness is an integral part of physical fitness. Achieving sexual fitness is a matter of extending one's physical sexual capabilities. TSFR will enable a normal, healthy man to both strengthen his potency and–in most cases–to prevent impotence; and remember that prevention is the best cure.

Who Can Learn TSFR?

Practically everyone can learn this technique. All it takes is a genuine desire and a little effort. Of course, as with any skill time and practice are also required. But the exercises themselves are not difficult. And this publication will guide you every step of the way.

The total time required to start benefiting from TSFR varies from individual to individual, depending on a person's age, health, and general physical condition. For example, it may take only a couple of months of regular daily practice for some healthy young man to achieve the full benefits of his TSFR program. On the other hand, for someone over 60 who has been impotent for several years, six months or longer may be required. In most cases, however, it takes about three months of regular daily practice to see the good results coming out of it. It should be mentioned that each daily practice session takes about 15 minutes only.

The point is that while it is easy to learn, TSFR does take time and regular practice. It would be misleading to imply that anyone will achieve "instant" results. But then nothing of lasting value is ever achieved in an instant.

Before You Begin . . .

Finally, before moving on to the actual details of the program, it is essential to say a word or two about approaching TSFR with the proper attitude and mental preparation. In many ways, each of us can be our own worst enemy. If we decide that something will not work, then in all probability, it will not work. An individual's attitude can be such an important factor that no program, however powerful, will be able to overcome it.

Certainly it is natural to be skeptical about TSFR. But it would be a serious mistake to dismiss it out of hand. It is a technique that has worked for countless men for centuries. And it can work for you, if you approach it with a positive attitude.

As mentioned earlier, TSFR like yoga or oriental martial arts involves both physical and mental conditioning. On the mental side of things, the most important point to remember is that you must relax. This is especially important when you are just beginning the program.

Your goal should be to relax, attempt an exercise, relax, and try again. Think of yourself as water flowing over and around the rock of the exercise you must accomplish. You are fluid, never brittle, relaxed. You offer no resistance, yet you flow. And should the rock refuse to yield, you return and flow over it again, and again, relaxed. And one day, almost of its own accord, the rock yields. And you flow on.

Be as persistent and patient–and relaxed–as that water. Commit yourself to the project. Practice the exercises faithfully and regularly. And you will succeed.

PART II: The TSFR Exercise
—Beginner's Training Program

We are going to present the beginner's training program of the TSFR exercise in two versions: original and modified versions. Because the original version is not easy to learn, the modified version is recommended. The modified version is just as effective as the original one. The important thing is to follow each instruction carefully and practice it correctly.

Immediately before each practice session, be sure to relax your mind and body; clear your mind of all thoughts, block out all outside distractions. Closing your eyes and thinking of nothing is the best way to prepare your mind and body for the exercise. The process will enable you to devote your full concentration to the exercise.

TSFR Exercise–The Original Version

Here are the steps to follow in practicing the original version of TSFR:

1. Kneel so that both knees are on the floor, all toes touching the floor, heels raised so that the soles face backward. Keep both knees comfortably apart on the floor.
2. Relax your body at this position. Hold the scrotum in your left hand and apply small amount of gentle pressure, (i.e. Hold and squeeze the scrotum very gently.)
3. Close your eyes. Slowly exhale through your mouth until there is almost no air left in your lungs. Then slowly inhale through your nose, making a deliberate effort to direct the air all the way down to Tan-Tien. (Tan-Tien is located at the lower part of your abdomen, about 3 inches below your navel.)
4. The inhaling process should last a few seconds. Once the lower part of your abdomen is "inflated," stop and hold your breath. At this point, still holding your breath, press the Fei-Ing, the spot located midway between the anus and the scrotum, with the central finger of your right hand and clinch your teeth. Put your tongue against the front roof of your mouth in order to tighten all the nerves.
5. At precisely this moment, contract the muscle of your anus with great effort and, keeping your

back straight, lean the upper part of your body forward slightly while pulling in your stomach. Then lower your buttocks until they are about 6 inches above the heels of your feet, but do not sit on your heels.

6. Hold your upper-body in this position, with the anus muscle contracted, for about 5 seconds. Then release the scrotum and relax your whole body by loosening all nerves and muscles. At the same time begin to release the air you've inhaled through your nose at first, then by blowing the remainder out through your mouth.

All of the actions described in steps 2 through 6 constitute one complete cycle. Relax for a few minutes before trying another complete cycle. You should perform 10 complete cycles in one practice session.

Although the time of day you select for your practice session is not as important as your regularity in practice, it is recommended that you practice either early in the morning soon after getting up and/or at night just before going to bed.

Also, it's important to realize that, while the exercise is presented in several steps above, these steps are simply a series of actions played in "slow motion" for the purpose of explanation. In reality, they constitute one smooth exercise. When you become familiar with various steps, the flow from one step to the next will become rhythmic and automatic. This is true for all other practice routines to be presented in this publication.

The Modified Version of TSFR Exercise

The original version presented above was developed as a special application of Chi Kung, a form of Kung Fu that has been practiced in China for thousands of years. If you happen to be an experienced Chi Kung practitioner, you undoubtedly found the original version of TSFR fairly easy to do.

But for people who do not practice Chi Kung, the control and manipulation of the breathing process may be somewhat difficult to learn and practice. It is for this reason that we have provided the following modified version of TSFR.

The exercises in the modified version can be performed in several different positions – sitting, standing, and lying positions. Each position is separately described on the following pages.

I. The Sitting Position

There are two variations of the sitting position (A) and (B):

The Sitting Position (A)

1. Begin by sitting squarely in a chair. The top

surface of the chair should be hard and it should be about as high as your knees.

Hold your chest out and, keeping your spine straight, lean your upper body forward to about 15 degrees forward of the vertical position.

Close your mouth. Stare with both of your eyes at an imaginary spot or an actual object lying on the floor about 3 to 4 feet in front of you.

2. Cross your legs; either leg may be on top.

Clasp both hands firmly against the knee belonging to the top leg, as shown in Figure 1. Then pull both hands against the knee toward your body with great effort.

While you are pulling both hands toward you, tighten all the nerves in your body. (The pulling action will help you accomplish this.)

3. At this moment, inhale gradually through your nose (Your mouth should still be closed). Don't breathe in too hard or too fast as this may strain the chest. When you have inhaled all the air you can hold, pull in your stomach, constrict your penis (like pulling the penis in), and contract the muscle of your anus all at the same time.

While you are contracting the muscle of your anus, you should be also pulling your anus upward such that your buttocks are almost about to rise from the top of the chair seat.

Hold your entire body and nerves in this contracted state for a few seconds until you feel the need to breathe again.

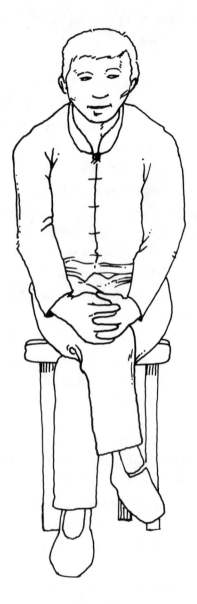

Figure 1.

Then open your mouth a little bit and exhale gradually. Release your hands from your knees, loosen up all the nerves and muscles in your body and return your upper body to the natural sitting position to relax.

This completes one full cycle. (One complete cycle takes about 15 seconds).

After completing one full cycle, rest and relax for a little while before starting another cycle.

Do 10 complete cycles in one practice session.

Since the constriction of the penis and contraction of the muscle of the anus are the most important part of the whole exercise process, we would like to elaborate upon this point further so that you can learn and practice this exercising routine correctly.

The action of constricting the penis is very much like that of trying to stop or trying to prevent the urine from coming out when you are urinating. In other words, it is the same as the action that shuts off the urinary stream. If you do it correctly you will be able to feel your penis physically pulling inward. (i.e. you can feel the sensation of the penis' pulling-back movement.) In the beginning the sensation may be weak, but it should become strong enough for you to feel it after you practice the routine for a while.

Similarly, the action of contracting the muscle of the anus and pulling the anus inward and upward is very much like the action of trying to stop the stool from coming out, which often occurs involuntarily when we are having a bowl movement. Particularly, at the end of the bowl movement, the anus often contracts and pulls inward involuntarily as if it tries to stop the residual stool from coming out. This holds true for all TSFR practice routines.

The Sitting Position (B)

The sitting position (A) described above is not suitable for those who have large stomachs. For those who find Sitting Position A uncomfortable, Sitting Position B provides an effective alternative.

1. Sit down on a chair as described for Sitting Position A. Hold your chest out and spine straight as you lean your upper body forward about 30 degrees away from the vertical position.

   Close your mouth. Stare with both of your eyes at a certain object of your choice lying on the floor about 3 to 4 feet in front of you. Separate your two feet and keep them comfortably apart.

2. Put both feet on the floor, but do not put any weight on your feet. Clasp both hands firmly together with effort and put the clasped hands slightly against the lower part of your abdomen –the part slightly above the penis, as shown in Figure 2.

3. Contract the muscle of your anus. At the same time pull your buttocks inward and upward in

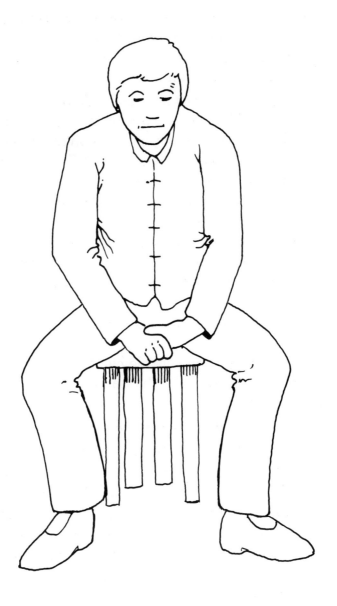

Figure 2.

such a way that it feels as if you are not sitting on the chair. You will actually be sitting on top of the chair, but with very little body weight pressing down upon it.

As you are contracting the muscle of the anus, you should also be constricting your penis. Hold your entire body in this contracted and constricted state for a few seconds. Then loosen up all the muscles and nerves and return your body to the natural sitting position and relax.

This completes one full cycle. The breathing process and other details are the same as those described in Sitting Position (A) above.

II. The Standing Position

When there is no suitable chair available, you can perform essentially the same exercise in a standing position.

1. Stand up straight, feet spread about a shoulder's width apart. Straighten your spine and open your shoulders. Lean your body about 15 degrees forward from the vertical position.
2. Clasp both hands firmly together with effort. Hold your clasped hands toward your body, and put them against your navel, as shown in Figure 3.
3. Pull your stomach in. Contract the muscle of your anus and pull it upward. At the same time, you should also be constricting your penis.

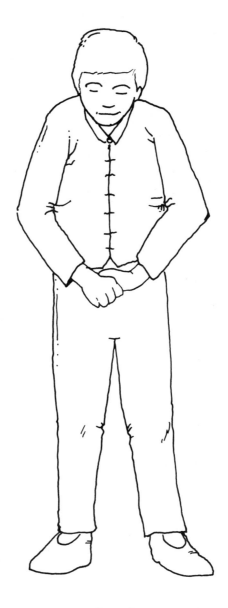

Figure 3.

From this point on, follow the same instructions for Sitting Position (B).

III. The Lying Position

TSFR may also be practiced in bed, in a lying position. This can be particularly convenient when you wake up in the morning and find that your penis has risen before you have. Before the erection disappears, do a few cycles of TSFR in the lying position. Once you get out of the bed, you can practice the sitting positions described above.

Here is the practice routine for TSFR in the lying position:

Lie on your side. Bend both legs at the knees. Cross your two hands in front of you and hold them against your chest. Pull the lower part of your abdomen in. Close your mouth and flare your nostrils in order to tighten the nerve in the nose.

This will enable you to concentrate on the contraction of the muscle of the anus and the constriction of the penis which have been previously described.

All other details are the same as those for the two sitting positions or the standing position.

As you've undoubtedly noticed, all three positions call for essentially the same set of inhalations, constrictions, and contractions. So long as you practice correctly and regularly, you may use any position you like. At the beginning, however, it is probably best to use one of the sitting positions.

At the first reading, you might get the impression that the modified version is as difficult to learn and practice as the original. Once you try these exercises, though, you'll find that they're a lot easier to perform than they appear. Not that learning the exercises won't take some practice. It will. But once your body and mind begin to work in a coordinated fashion, the exercises will come naturally. Again, all it takes is a willingness to try and a little patience.

It's also important to point out that all of the exercise routines described above are designed for the beginner. The intent is to help him learn the basic techniques correctly—especially the proper way to contract the muscle of the anus while simultaneously constricting the penis. Once you've learned this basic technique, you will be able to advance to the TSFR Regular Practice Routine described below.

If you are impotent, the continued practice of the beginner's training routines, plus the complementary massages described in the next section of this manual, will enable you to gain an erection. Frequently this will occur when you wake up in the morning. Not that waking up with an erection is unusual. It's just that continued practice of the beginner's training routines will cause it to happen with greater frequency.

When you notice this happening on a fairly regular basis, it is a sign that your TSFR training is having the desired effect. And it means that it is time to conduct a self-test to determine whether you should move on to the TSFR Regular Practice Routine.

Once you have learned the technique, when you contract the muscle of your anus, your penis will automatically "pull in" by itself and the muscle of the penis will also "stretch" and "expand" involuntarily. In other words, the contraction of the muscle of your anus will cause your penis to "pull in" and "stretch" and "expand" involuntarily. This is the thing to observe in the self-test just mentioned above.

Here is the simple procedure for the self-test. When you wake up with a good erection, hold the shaft of your hard penis with your right hand. Breathe in gradually and naturally and then breathe out gradually also. Near the end of the breathing out process contract the muscle of your anus and see if you can clearly feel the penis physically "pull in" and also "stretch" and "expand" in your right hand. If you can feel this, you have passed the self-test.

Some people will probably be able to pass this self-test after they have practiced the Beginner's Training Program for only a few weeks. In any event, advancing to the TSFR Regular Practice Routine will enable you to perform TSFR conveniently in a few minutes just after you wake up, while you are still in bed. It will be the only TSFR practice session you need each day.

The TSFR Regular Practice Routine

When you awake with an erection, lie in a comfortable position and hold the shaft of your penis with the first three fingers of your hand. Breathe in gradually and naturally and then breathe out gradually as well. When you are almost out of breath, contract the muscle of your anus while simultaneously constricting your penis.

In the course of this contracting/constricting process, you will definitely feel your penis involuntarily stretching and pulling at the same time. This completes one cycle.

You should practice 36 consecutive cycles. This will take less than a total of 4 minutes.

Once mastered, the contracting motion will become essentially involuntary and will require virtually no effort. If you do not wake up with an erection once in a while, for one reason or another, you should use your hand to stiffen your penis before practicing the TSFR routine. For a variety of reasons, it is more effective to practice TSFR when the penis is hard.

This involuntary "stretching" and "expanding" (flexing) of your penis due to the contraction of the muscle of your anus is very similar to the sensation you experience immediately after ejaculation during intercourse. As you will recall, at that point the penis typically continues to throb involuntarily several times before the erection disappears. As we'll see later, this is why the TSFR technique will enable you to control the real ejaculation during intercourse and help your partner achieve orgasm(s).

Please remember that regular TSFR practice is essential. You should practice this simple routine every morning unless you can not do so physically for reasons beyond your control.

PART III:
The Complementary TSFR Massages

In addition to the TSFR exercises described above, there is a set of massages developed by the Taoist for helping a man achieve complete sexual fitness. Although these massages can be used independently of TSFR for strengthening your sexual potency, they are most effective when they are practiced as part of a total TSFR program. Together the massages and TSFR exercise are the most powerful combination of the Taoist techniques for achieving the sexual fitness.

The complementary massages will be particularly helpful for those who are 45 years of age or older and for those who suffer from impotence.

1. Tan-Tien and Inguinal Massages

Stand up on the floor with your feet about twelve inches apart. Rub your palms against each other until they feel warm. Then use the palm of your left hand to hold the penis and scrotum and use the palm of your right hand to massage (press and rub) the right side of inguinal region (i.e. the root portion of your right leg where the right leg joins the right side of your lower abdomen).

Perform this massage rather forcefully back and forth 36 times. Then change hands. Use the palm of your right hand to hold the penis and scrotum and use the palm of your left hand to massage the left side of inguinal region. See Figure 4.1.

Then go on to massage the Tan-Tien (located at the lower part of your abdomen, about 3 inches below the navel). Use your left hand to hold your penis and pull it outward while using the palm of your right hand to massage the Tan-Tien with strength, rotating from right to left 36 times.

Then change hands. Use your right hand to hold your penis and pull it outward while using the palm of your left hand to massage the Tan-Tien as described above. Please see Figure 4.2.

Although you should massage these areas with strength, you should not, of course, press and rub the areas so hard that you hurt the skin. The proper massage technique is a slow, firm rubbing motion that includes a moderate amount of pressure.

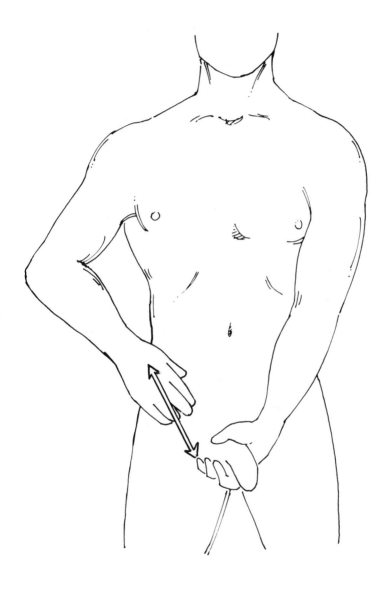

Figure 4.1

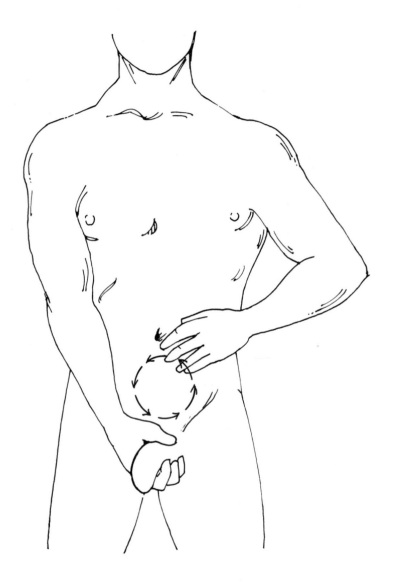

Figure 4.2

2. Kidney-Area Massage

Rub the palms of your hands against each other as you did for the previous massage. Then use the warm palms to rub the parts of your lower back (right palm on the right side of your back, left palm on the left side) directly above the kidneys. Do this 36 times. Please see Figure 5.

3. Fuey-Ing Massage

Fuey-Ing is a delicate spot located midway between the scrotum and anus. First, rub the palms of your hands against each other until heat is produced. Set your legs apart and bend your knees as if you are riding a horse. Use your left hand to hold your penis and scrotum and use the four fingers (except the thumb) of your right hand together to gently massage Fuey-Ing back and forth for 36 times.

You must remember that Fuey-Ing massage must be gentle. Don't press and rub Fuey-Ing too hard so that you won't hurt this delicate spot. Fuey-Ing massage can also be done when you are lying in bed. The procedure is the same as above.

4. Inner Thigh Massage

Rub the palms of your hands against each other until heat is produced. Then use the warm palm of

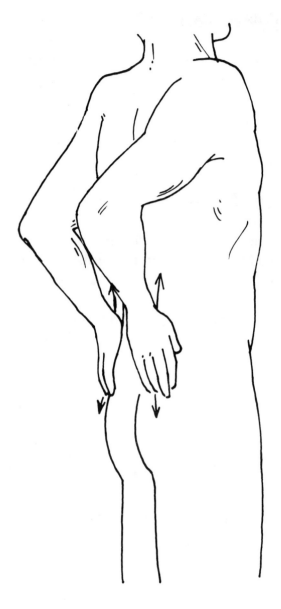

Figure 5.

your right hand to rub with strength the inner thigh of your right leg from the inguinal part all the way down to the inner part of your right knee and back up again to the inguinal part. Rub this way down and up again for 36 times. Then use the palm of your left hand to rub the inner thigh of your left leg in exactly the same way for 36 times.

5. Head and Neck Massages

Rub the palms of your hands until heat is produced. Then use the warm palm to massage the nape of your neck and the back of your head (with the palm of your right hand on the nape of your neck and the palm of your left hand on the back of your head). Massage this way back and forth for 36 times. Then change hands and repeat 36 times. Please see Figure 6.1.

Next, go on to massage your head with fingers of both hands from the forehead up and along and around the top of the head and down to the back of your head. Massage your head this way for 36 times, as illustrated in Figure 6.2.

Then cover your ears with your palms with fingers of both hands laying on the back of your head. Cross the index finger over the middle finger on both hands and snap down your index finger to strike the back of your head on both sides (the right index finger snaps and strikes the right side of the back of your head and the left index finger snaps

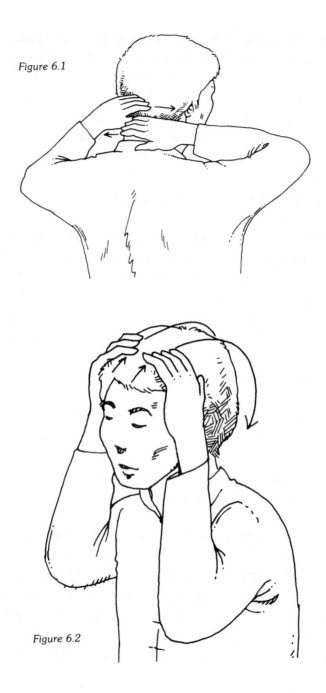

Figure 6.1

Figure 6.2

42

and strikes the left side). Repeat 36 times. Please see Figure 6.3.

6. Pubic Region Massage

Use the fingers (except thumbs) of both of your hands to press the area around the root of the penis and the general pubic region. Press firmly each time and hold for a few seconds.

Start with the upper part of the region and move down to the lower part of the region, spot-by-spot. Then move to the left side and right side of the area.

In the beginning perform this pressing massage for about 5 minutes. The time and firmness of the pressing action can be gradually increased. Besides the pressing massage just mentioned, rubbing the area around the root of the penis is also very important. So make sure you also practice the rubbing action.

Before leaving this section, it's important to point out that this set of massages is essential for strengthening your sexual potency. These massages are designed to invigorate the nervous system that controls the sexual functions and to maintain the healthy normal secretion of sexual hormones.

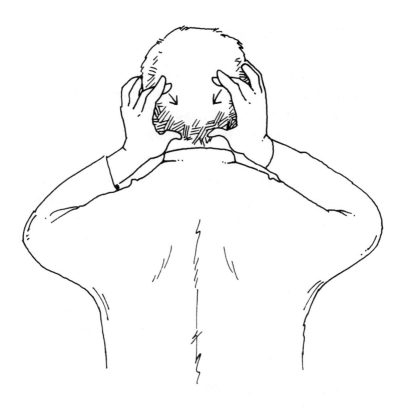

Figure 6.3

Be sure to practice them every day in the morning soon after you get up and at night before you go to bed. Each session will take only about 15 minutes.

PART IV:
Increasing Staying Power through TSFR

In this section we'll look at how TSFR can be used to both overcome the problem of premature ejaculation and to increase the length of time any man can maintain an erection.

However, before presenting the relevant TSFR details, let's look briefly at some of the clinical techniques for preventing or curing premature ejaculation.

As we mentioned in the beginnng section of this manual, any ejaculation that occurs before you or your partner desire it is "premature." Some specific severe cases of premature ejaculation are ejaculations before intromission, at intromission, or within seconds of intromission. A person with this kind of ejaculation problem is often considered a rapid ejaculator. Premature ejaculation usually results from inexperience, prolonged abstinence, or for psychological reasons.

Of course, weak potency will also lead to premature ejaculation. By far the most common psychological reason is the performance anxiety which results from the fear of premature ejaculation. Chances are, if you worry about ejaculating too soon, that is exactly what will happen. Clearly this is a psychological problem, and it is important to recognize it as such so that you will not let it stand in your way.

Before we discuss the TSFR techniques for the prevention of premature ejaculation it is important to recognize that there exists a point of "ejaculatory inevitability" in the course of sexual intercourse. Male sexual arousal is a voluntary response up to this point. But beyond this point the response becomes involuntary and a man will ejaculate no matter what he or his partner does.

Generally, when you begin to feel the sensation of the penis being "full" and the urge to release the ejaculation, you are imminently approaching this point. In learning any technique for preventing premature ejaculation it is necessary to become more aware of this sensation and to learn to control the intensity of sexual stimulation in order to prevent oneself from going beyond this point.

Furthermore, it is appropriate to mention a few basic points that are helpful in delaying the male orgasm during intercourse in order to achieve better sexual satisfaction as follows:

Point 1. Relax and learn to pace yourself. Take your time. Do not rush. Do not be anxious. Obviously this is easier said than done, but it is a goal worth striving for. Gradually you will be able to relax and pace yourself.

Point 2. Be tender and loving with your partner. Be sure to permit her the time she needs to get ready for you. Extended foreplay is often the most effective way to do this. And, always, genuine partner-to-partner communication is essential to first class love making. Try to find out what really turns her on so that you can help her to get ready effectively. You could experiment any stimulating techniques you can imagine. Use your hand and your tongue creatively. Besides getting her ready for intercourse, sex play before penetration has a lot of fun in its own right. So, take time to play it and enjoy it; don't rush into intercourse and miss the fun of foreplay.

Point 3. Let the foreplay eventually take both of you to intercourse naturally. Upon penetration, hold your penis still inside of her and take a couple of deep breaths and do some little things such as massaging your neck in the back or tickling your ears, etc. in order to ease the tension and excitement generated during the process of penetration.

Don't hurry on to the thrusting motion right after penetration because at the moment of entry the sexual tension is usually high and you need to cool it down for a little while before you go on to a thrusting motion.

Once you start the thrusting motion don't keep on stroking without a break. After a few strokes you should stop for a break and take a couple of deep breaths and do some little things that will ease the tension a little. There is no definite time interval regarding when to stop for a break. This depends on each individual. The basic idea is to stop for a break long before the point of ejaculatory inevitability (PEI).

You have to try some experiments to find out what is the proper interval for yourself. For example, if it usually takes you 10 strokes to reach PEI once you start the thrusting motion, you should then try to stop for a break after you have completed 6 or 7 strokes. If you wait until you start to feel the urge to release it, it is probably too late. We should mention here that if at any time you reach the PEI earlier than you want it don't worry and don't be upset, just relax and let it go and allow yourself to enjoy the ejaculation. You can always try again to control it next time.

Remember, the learning process is basically a trial and error process. During the learning process it is easier to try slow, rhythmic, non-demanding thrusting, because it is more difficult to control with rapid thrusting, especially in the male superior position.

Also, in the beginning you, of course, need the support and cooperation of your partner. The approach we just describe here will definitely help you prolong the intercourse for better sexual fulfillment.

Point 4. The mental ability to switch your mind from intercourse to something else can help you delay the climax and prolong the intercourse. Practically, every man can develop this ability if he sets his mind to it and practices the various simple tricks described below.

Of course, it takes time and practice to develop this ability. The basic idea is to direct your attention to something else instead of intercourse in order to ease the tension. For example, you may think of something interesting which happened in the office or on the golf course, or simply memorizing the multiplication table in your mind when you are stroking inside of her. This will shift your attention away from physical sensations of intercourse temporarily.

The mental power of turning your attention to something else will usually last only a little while. Therefore you have to intersperse this attention-shifting trick with periodic physical motions of some sort.

For example, you can have your partner tickle your ears, your armpit, etc. or have her pull your ears or your hair a little bit. These kinds of little things will draw your attention away from intercourse temporarily in order to ease the mounting tension. Physical movement of certain parts of your body during intercourse, such as changing the intercourse position slightly or completely (e.g. move your legs up and down, cross or bend your legs, or completely roll over, etc.) will also draw your attention away from love making temporarily.

In fact, changing from position to position among those positions she likes during the intercourse is often a simple and effective way of diffusing tension and prolonging the intercourse. Another trick is to use the fingers of your left hand (or right hand) to scratch the sole of your left foot (or right foot) strenuously and, at the same time, clinch your teeth and stare fiercely at those things surrounding you with your eyes when the tension starts to mount.

This trick requires that you bend your knee and turn your upper body in such a way that your hand can reach the sole of your foot. If it is uncomfortable for you to try this trick, you can just forget about it, because there are quite a few other tricks you can use as we have just mentioned above.

To sum this point up, the basic idea is to deliberately slow down when the tension starts to mount and start again once the tension is subsided.

With these four basic points in mind let us turn our attention now to several specific techniques for preventing premature ejaculation. Before we do so, we would like to mention that the four basic points described above are obviously not Taoist techniques. Some readers undoubtedly have heard about some of these basic points before. They are reviewed here because they are helpful in controlling the male orgasm during intercourse. As such, they are applicable to and should be employed in conjunction with any one of the following techniques:

1. The TSFR Technique

Once you have learned the TSFR technique described in the previous section, you should use it during intercourse to control your ejaculation and prolong your love-making. This technique is probably the most effective technique for controlling ejaculation. When you use it you must still follow all the basics described above.

Upon penetration, hold your penis still inside her and take a couple of deep breaths for a break. Then breathe in gradually and naturally and breathe out gradually, too. Near the end of the breathing out contract the muscle of your anus and constrict (pull in) your penis at the same time as if you deliberately try to prevent ejaculation. (In other words, you just practice the TSFR exercise at this moment.)

Do this TSFR contraction 3 times. Then go on to the stroking motion using the basic described in Point 3 above. During each break, do this TSFR contraction a few times. By exercising this TSFR technique during each timed break, you can delay ejaculation and continue intercourse virtually indefinitely. This way you can help your partner achieve orgasm after orgasm until finally you decide to join her in a mutual climax.

The TSFR exercises you perform during each break will not only prevent premature ejaculation but also cause your penis to flex and throb inside your partner, allowing you to provide your partner with a special, pleasure-heightening sensation. It is a sensation that can be so powerful that multiple female orgasms may result.

We would like to mention another important point in love making. Women are much slower to descend from the plateau of sexual excitement than men. The man will often collapse in satisfied exhaustion, while his partner remains partially aroused. Consequently, you should not withdraw too soon after ejaculation. Instead, continue to exercise the TSFR contraction.

Meanwhile, she can manipulate her body to give the penis some pressure in order to slow down its retreat. The continued exercise of the TSFR contraction will prevent the penis from wilting too soon so that you can give her time to come down from the climax in a very satisfying tender-loving way. In fact, you should also exercise gentle caressing, kissing, or holding each other to enable the pleasure to last much longer. This will make both of you truly satiated at the end!

Of course, it requires practice to be able to use the TSFR technique effectively in controlling the ejaculation. In the beginning you might not be able to control the ejaculation effectively when you apply the technique. But it would not take long before you gain enough experience to be able to control the ejaculation effectively during inter-course. And continued practice of this technique will eventually enable you to control the ejaculation at will and to prolong the intercourse as long as you want.

TSFR is a truly amazing technique. In fact, if you wish you can control yourself not to come at all while you could give her full satisfaction with multiple orgasms.

The ancient Taoist held that semen was a very precious "spiritual essence." So their philosophy was that a man should be careful to conserve semen by not ejaculating as much as he can. This seems to run against the western culture where people consider that while long intercourse is great, the aim is to ejaculate eventually. Therefore, we would not advise you to conserve your semen by controlling it from coming. But it is nice to know that this can be done with the TSFR technique, if necessary.

2. Testicles-Squeezing Technique

This is a technique for treating impotence as well as for developing the ability to maintain a long intercourse. You can practice this technique when you take a warm-water bath. The procedure is fairly simple.

Submerge your body in the warm water in a bath tub (or in a hot tub, if you have one). Use your hand to hold and squeeze the testicles firmly for a few seconds. Then release them by opening your hand abruptly. Repeat the squeezing and releasing actions for a dozen times.

After several squeezes the penis will probably begin to stiffen. However it will not become too hard since it is submerged in the warm water. Then use both hands to squeeze, twist, and massage the hardened penis slowly as if you were masturbating. As the tension mounts, stop squeezing and massaging. Once the tension has eased, you can resume.

You can apply the attention-shifting trick described in Point 4 above to avoid ejaculating. Remember, this entire process of squeezing and massaging the penis is performed in the warm water.

3. Penis-Squeezing Technique

This is a technique for developing the first class erection and the ability to prolong the intercourse. The procedure is also pretty simple. Sit on the edge of the bed (or a chair) with both feet stepped on the toes and both heels raised from the floor so that your hand can easily reach the Fei-Ing (located midway between the anus and scrotum).

Use the middle three fingers of your left hand to press the Fei-Ing firmly and the right hand to squeeze your penis firmly and hold for several seconds. Then release both hands from the Fei-Ing and penis.

This completes one cycle. Do 36 cycles in a row. Whenever the tension mounts during the process, stop the action. When the tension is subsided, begin again.

4. Desensitizing and Drilling Technique

This technique provides a good training for overcoming the trouble of ejaculating too quickly upon penetration because of lack of sexual experience, particularly for young men. The procedure is rather simple.

Use your left hand to hold the lower part of the shaft of the penis and the right hand to squeeze and massage the glans and the upper part of the shaft of the penis with a small clean dry towel as if you were masturbating. The squeezing and massaging action will stiffen your penis.

You should use those tricks described in Points 3 and 4 during this process to practice the ability of deliberately avoiding the ejaculation. Whenever the tension mounts you should stop squeezing and massaging (i.e. masturbating) action. When the tension has eased, resume the action again. Continued practice of this technique will help to desensitize the tip of your penis, for a slower sexual "trigger." Sometimes, a clean fine painting brush can also be used to brush the glans in an effort to desensitize it.

In this section we have described quite a few techniques for developing the ability to control the ejaculation and to prolong intercourse. You may just concentrate on practicing the TSFR technique alone. But if you have any impotence problems you should also practice the testicles-squeezing and penis-squeezing techniques as well.

Or if you are a rapid ejaculator you should practice the desensitizing and drilling technique in addition to the TSFR technique. In any event the important requirement from you is to put them into practice. Continued regular practice of these techniques will eventually enable you to control ejaculation at will.

One common phenomenon that we should mention here is that many men simply will not be able to control the ejaculation when they have intercourse with a new partner for the first time or when they resume sexual intercourse with their regular partner after a prolonged abstinence. This is purely due to psychological reasons and is only a temporary phenomenon.

Another thing we should mention is that sex should be a spontaneous event. It should not be planned or pre-meditated. If you premeditate and anticipate sex you are simply building up subconsciously the sexual anxiety that will make you come quickly when you finally get there.

Again, this is purely a psychological problem and is only temporary. So, if it sometimes happens to you, don't worry about it. When you try again the problem will disappear.

PART V:
Putting TSFR to Work for You

Now that we have described the entire spectrum of TSFR techniques, let us turn to a few things that you ought to keep in mind as you put it into practice:

1. During the first month of TSFR training you should try to minimize the number of times of intercourse. If you can avoid the intercourse completely that would be even better.

   During the second month you can gradually increase the frequency of intercourse. After the first couple of months you will no longer need to refrain from sex. And once you have developed TSFR skills you will be able to enjoy sex literally as often as you want.

Refraining from sex during the first couple of months of training is not much of a price to pay for this capability. And we feel you should do so.

If you come too quickly when you resume intercourse after several weeks of abstinence, you should realize that this is purely psychological and the problem will quickly pass.

2. Moderate and regular TSFR exercise with its complementary massages is the best way to achieve and maintain sexual fitness. Don't just practice once or twice a week with three or four times as many cycles as prescribed in the training section. Do not, for example, do not try 100 or more cycles in one practice session because you missed the practice for a few days and are trying to compensate.

   This kind of irregular and strenuous exercise is not only ineffective but also could be harmful. Be sure to follow the instructions closely and carefully. In the beginning practice once in the morning after you get up and once at night before you go to bed every day and each time practice 10 cycles as described in the training section.

   The number of cycles practiced each time can be gradually increased week by week until it reaches 36 cycles. It is not necessary to do more than 36 cycles in each practice session. Your goal should be to learn the technique gradually so that your body can become accustomed to the exercise without strain.

3. While sexual fitness is an integral part of physical fitness, the term physical fitness obviously covers a much broader area. Thus it goes without saying that you should not neglect other kinds of exercise that are good for your general physical fitness, particularly if you are 50 years of age or older.

Once you reach middle age it is important that you put all your muscles and joints through a full range of movement every day. For older people, therefore, we strongly recommend stretching your muscles and joints (e.g. neck, shoulders, elbows, hands, hips, knees and feet) through some soft flexibility exercises after your daily TSFR practice routine.

If you don't know what kind of soft stretching exercise you can do in the morning, consult a doctor, physiotherapist, or physical education teacher.

Summary of TSFR Benefits

Once you developed TSFR skills, the daily regimen of TSFR exercise and its complementary massages will enable you to achieve and maintain complete sexual fitness for the rest of your life. Specifically, TSFR will enable you to:

-Improve potency
-Increase "muscle-like" tone of the penis

-Gain a first-class erection
-Prevent impotence
-Control ejaculation during intercourse
-Prevent premature ejaculation
-Assist your partner in achieving orgasm(s)

Psychologically, TSFR instills confidence in you. TSFR will enable you to gain complete self-confidence and self-esteem. Confidence is a very important key to solving both impotence and premature ejaculation problems. Armed with the TSFR technique and the tips on love-making mentioned in this manual, you will be able to improve your sexual performance, and the improvement will reinforce your confidence.

The more confident you become, the greater the improvement you will achieve. Before long, you will be a man with the great virility that you have always wanted. Not only will you be proud of your own achievement, you will also be loved dearly by your partner for your special ability. You will definitely feel an increased sense of general well-being, more vitality and zest for life.

CONCLUSION

There is an old Chinese saying that food and sex are the two most natural desires as well as the two most essential needs. Furthermore, the hallmark of the philosophy of Taoism has always been to seek the best things in life through the simplest and most natural means. It is thus easy to understand why the ancient Taoist were motivated to develop this secret sexual regimen in their quest for naturally increased sexual satisfaction.

Today, we are grateful for their efforts since, like countless fortunate individuals over the centuries, we too can now enjoy the benefits of TSFR.

A healthy and robust sex life is a beautiful facet of a fulfilling life. You deserve all the pleasure sex has to offer. It is perfectly natural, normal, and healthy to want to perform better sexually. You should congratulate yourself on being so lucky to get hold of the priceless information contained in this manual. The best way to cherish this information is to put it into use for yourself. We are sure that eventually you will realize that this manual is one of the best things you ever received in your life. We sincerely believe that by publishing this manual we are performing a great service to mankind. And we feel certain that the Taoist would have approved whole heartedly of this effort.

Finally we would like to conclude this with a sacred request:

Whoever uses or quotes the Taoist techniques contained in this manual, no matter in which way and in what formats, expression, or languages, should always give the due credit and respect to the ancient Taoist; no one should try to take the credit of inventing these remarkable Taoist techniques away from the ancient Taoist and claim the credit of the invention for himself. Eventually, the countless readers of this manual will be the judges for any violator of this sacred request.

–END–

THE TSFR SURVEY

As mentioned in the introduction, we have initiated a project to collect the actual personal experiences of the readers of this manual.

The purposes of the project are to evaluate the effectiveness of the TSFR based upon feedback from the readers who have faithfully practiced it and to document the "official" evidence to support the claims for TSFR contained in this manual. As such, it is a moral responsibility and worthwhile cause for the reader to participate in this project. You are, therefore, sincerely asked to complete this survey and return it to us at the appropriate time.

The appropriate time is defined as one of the following two cases as it applies to you individually:

(a) When you have realized good results from practicing TSFR

(b) When you still have not realized any good results at all even though you have faithfully and regularly practiced TSFR for twelve months.

Although you may mail the completed survey in pseudo-nymously/anonymously, you should use your real address, for upon its receipt we will place you on our mailing list of TSFR practitioners. The mailing list is to be used for disseminating further information on TSFR released by the Golden Dragon Publishers, Inc. in the future.

1. Name _____

2. Address: City_____State_____Zip_____

3. Personal Data: Age_____Height_____

   Weight_____Marital Status_____
   If not married, do you have a regular partner: ☐ Yes ☐ No
   Health _____(e.g. excellent, good, etc.)
   (Please indicate significant medical problems, e.g. diabetes, stomach ulcer, etc.)

4. Overall, would you conclude that TSFR does work for you?
   ☐ Yes ☐ No

5. Do you smoke? ☐ Yes ☐ No
   If you do, how many packs of cigarettes a day on the average do you smoke?
   > ☐ less than one pack
   > ☐ less than two packs
   > ☐ more than two packs

6. Alcohol consumption: Please check one of the following as an indication of your daily alcohol consumption in terms of number of drinks per day on the average.
   ☐ equivalent to less than 1 drink a day
   ☐ equivalent to less than 2 drinks a day
   ☐ equivalent to less than 5 drinks a day
   ☐ equivalent to less than 10 drinks a day
   ☐ equivalent to more than 10 drinks a day

7. How many equivalent months of daily regular practice of TSFR did it take you to start getting good results and benefiting from it?
   > Equivalent to _____ months.

8. Did you have impotence problems before you started practicing TSFR?
   ☐ Yes ☐ No

If yes, was it:
- ☐ partial impotence?
- ☐ total impotence?

Do you now still have any impotence problem? ☐ Yes ☐ No

Overall, did TSFR strengthen your potency? ☐ Yes ☐ No

9. Has TSFR helped you prolong intercourse and gain more sexual enjoyment and satisfaction? ☐ Yes ☐ No
(Please feel free to elaborate on your progress in the space below.)

10. Do you do other exercise for your general physical fitness?
☐ Yes ☐ No
If yes, what kind of exercise?
☐ Jogging   ☐ Racquetball   ☐ Tennis   ☐ Swimming
or other (please specify) _____

Please use the space below for your further comments, if any.

May we quote you?   ☐ Yes   ☐ No

Please return the completed survey to:
BRUCE WONG
c/o Golden Dragon Publishers, Inc.
P.O. BOX 1529
PRINCETON, NEW JERSEY 08540